T0198888

SHIPS IN BOTTLES

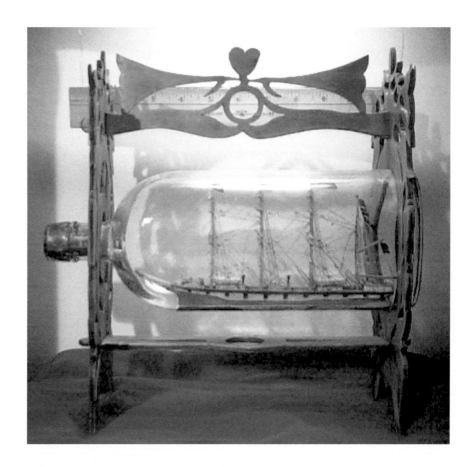

A Ship-in-a-Bottle, the essence of the sea encapsulated and preserved for all time.
This is a look at a few of those marvelous, enchanting, original and unique works of the
sailor's art. These are the bottles that do not have to be opened, to enjoy the contents.

TEXT AND PHOTOGRAPHS BY LEO P. CONVERY SR.

Book Designer: Diana Seciu

To order additional copies of this book, contact:
Xlibris
844-714-8691
www.Xlibris.com
Orders@Xlibris.com

ISBN: Softcover   978-1-4134-2369-3

Library of Congress Control Number: 2003095385

Print information available on the last page

Rev. date: 04/03/2023

PICTURES OF A COLLECTION OF SHIPS-IN-BOTTLES.

All text and photos by Leo P. Convery

The bottles shown in this book span 60 years of collecting. Most come from the United States but about 12 came from England. Quite possibly some found in the U. S. may have been built In England or Europe or elsewhere. There is seldom any way to identify the country of origin or the builder. Some of the model ships fly country flags. This may only identify the ship was of that country. It may or may not identify the country of the builder. The bottles too traveled all over the world with the original contents so knowing the country of the bottler does not help identify the country of the maker or the ship or the age of the model as the bottle may be old and remain empty for years, until spotted by the model builder.

I have lived by the sea on an Island off Cape Cod, Massachusetts. The area was settled by sea-farers from early explorers to whalers and is now a favorite sailing destination. I have always been fas-cinated by sea stories and sea lore. Admiring and collecting marine antiques is a hobby and a pastime.

I hope you will enjoy this little book and the fine ships in bottles, with a glimpse into the Old Days of sailing ships on deep-sea voyages.

May 30, 2003

INTRODUCTION

Since man has been at sea there has been a fascination with ships especially sailing ships from the great square-riggers or tall ships to the weekend boat. Models of these vessels have probably been made from time the first ship was built. When sailors have time away from the hard work that goes into sailing and maintaining a vessel, they are drawn to dreaming about the sea and ships. If they happen to be artistic, and handy with tools, they build ship models for small boys or gifts for the men and women in their lives.

The *ship–in-a-bottle* offered a very unique challenge. How can they get a ship inside a bottle and get it to look as if it was built in place. The ship-in-a-bottle artist required a steady hand, a good eye and great patience. There are many good Ship-in-a-bottle model builders today, and a few are very talented artists. The World Wide Web has made it easy to find them. They exist in almost every country. Just go and type in "ship in a bottle" at any search engine and you will be amazed at the talent you will find.

HISTORY

The history of building Ship-in-a-bottles goes back at least 200 to 250 years. There are no records but from surviving art forms, it is possible to approximate beginnings. There are examples existing in museums of intricate scale models of miniature gold mines in a bottle. These date back to 1744. While not ship-in a- bottles, they illustrate that the idea was born to put things other than liquids in the bottles. The earliest ship-in-a-bottle in existence was built in 1784 by an Italian, Gioni Biondo. He put the date on one of the sails. The model is in the Museum of Arts and Culture in Lubeck, Germany. Probably the age of ship-in-a-bottle building came into its most prolific stage between 1850's to the 1940's. Most of what we consider antique ship-in-a-bottles comes from this period.

Back then, sailors had time to devote to craft work. The days at sea were long and hard but there were also long periods of boredom. Most early scrimshaw or bone and whale teeth carving were done at sea by whale-men on 2 and 3 years voyages. Active and busy hands kept the men out of shipboard mischief. Between trips, time was plentiful; there was no TV or other sources of amusement and activities as we enjoy today. Sailors and fishermen used the long cold idle winter for over hauling the gear. Then, if he was handy, carving or building models. Some models were made by prisoners-of-war. They, being incarcerated for long periods of time without adequate maintenance, would create marvelous things of wood, bone and glass to sell to be able to afford some little luxury. Other craftsmen were retired seamen or artists who were just fascinated by the subject. I remember at the age of 8 or 9 visiting an old man, a retired fisherman, who made ship-in-a-bottles while living a very large catboat up on land. Most Bottle models are one of a kind. Good antique models today are just scarce and hard to find. It is a craft type industry, and the supply is very limited. People, who own them, seem to hold on to them.

CONTEMPORARY MODELERS

Contemporary models of any originality or skilled execution exist in almost every country in the world. There are Ship-in-Bottles Associations in America, France, Denmark and Japan that I know of, so there must be others. Some of these people will build to your specification, and do magnificent custom work. In Japan there is a great many ship-in-bottle modelers, their work is exquisite and original. There are artists in Japan who create the most intricate, delicate background paintings that show one scene on the inside of the bottle and a different one on the out side. As much as I admire the work of these contemporary modelers, and even though the new work is beautifully executed, there is nothing like finding an antique old ship-in-a-bottle treasure in antique shops or private estate sales.

WHY?

Why did they do it? The ship-in-a-bottle offers two simple challenges! Can it be done? And, can I do it.? It might be the old timers also enjoyed a drink or two and had a lot of empty bottles kicking around. There is an amazing amount of different bottles that were put into service. Large, small, tall, fat, dimpled, pinched, rectangular, square and oval, there seems to be no one shape or size that proved un-useable. I have seen just about every size and shape utilized. One new Model maker will even do one in a light bulb or miniatures in a perfume bottle.

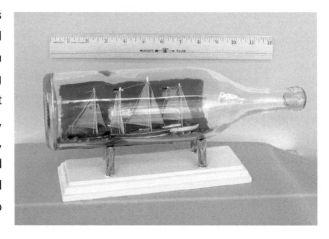

How is it done?

Basically it is a task of detailed planning and careful assembly. The great square-riggers and galleons are probably the most difficult ships to execute particularly in a small bottle. The builder has to make his own tools, engineer his own technique to get it all to fit together. First either the Bottle is chosen, then the ship type, or if for a specific ship, then the bottle is sought out that will fit. The neck opening will control how it can be inserted, therefore, any plan must adapt to this opening. Once the ship type and bottle is settled upon, a scale drawing is sketched out, and the hull cut to shape and size. The ship is completely assembled, painted and rigged outside of the bottle.

There are two methods for getting the ship into the bottle. In the first method, the masts have to have the ability to lay flat back toward the stern of the vessel if the bow is to point out toward the neck. Some builders build the mast attached to the vessel's deck by a wire hinge to allow them to pivot back flat. If sails are used, the sails must also be able to go flat and/or turn in a line sideways to fit through the neck. Once the bottle is ready to receive the ship, the fully rigged and finished ship is prepared by laying the masts flat, gathering the sails by rolling or folding them into a bundle that will fit through the neck into the bottle all at once. All the fore stays run from the forward mast to and through the bowsprit and are left long to reach well out of the bottle neck.

The bottle is prepared during the ship construction, with clay or putty for the sea, in the base of what will be, the bottom of the bottle. This is shaped and painted and dried. Any décor is added such as lighthouses or a village. The ship is then inserted into the bottle with the mast(s) flat and the hull is glued into the putty base. Larger hulls may have to be in two or even three pieces to fit through the bottle's neck. All of this is done by working through the bottle's neck with long and awkward custom tools. Once the glue is set and the model hull will hold in place, the builder attempts to pull on the fore stay strings to get the masts to raise up to vertical and set in place. No easy task. Once the masts are upright and sails are in place, the fore stays are glued in place on the bowsprit then the extra line is cut off

The second insertion method involves building the model out side of the bottle as in the first method, then disassembling the model and erecting it again piece by piece inside the bottle. Neither one is easy.

WHAT MAKES A GOOD *SHIP-IN-A-BOTTLE?*

What do I look for in a good ship in a bottle? It has been said "beauty is in the eye of the beholder". If it pleases you then it has done its work. I look first at the overall effect, is it pleasing, is the bottle simple or unique in shape. Is the Vessel unusual, one mast, or more, with sails? Or without? Bare masts and yards, furled or full sails? Was it difficult to rig, is it well situated. What is the setting? Is it a simple  water scene or elaborate landscape with a small village? Can the nationality of the ship be determined? Is the ship itself identifiable? Is there one ship or more? What is the stopper ? Is it a plain cork? Or is it a unique or intricate piece of sailors rope work? Or course if you already have one of one type of ship-in-a-bottle in your collection you may be looking for a different shape or different rigged vessel to complement it. The stand or display board is not as important as you can always make them. If it is well crafted and unique it will add to the value. Many a Ship-in-a-bottle I have found with just awful stands and wonder why, after so much work; was this stuck on a board with a couple of nails sticking up to hold the bottle? I once bought a beautiful Haig and Haig Pinch Bottle with a great 3-mast full sail square-rigger for very very cheap. It was attached to a plain flat board with glue. The board made up part of the most awful lamp; built either by a kid with a toy kit and no real tools or a guy with two left hands. The antique dealer was glad to get rid of it. Once I got it loose from the board, I had a great ship-in-a-bottle.

As you will see on turning the following pages, there are all types and sizes and great variety of interior scenes and ships of all descriptions. They defy classification or rating as for best or most skilled, each is unique in its own way.

I prefer the Haig and Haig pinch bottles as a form of display a bit above the rest. The pinch bottle itself is a pleasing form, and with a well done ship inside they just stand out. It just presents a very delightful overall image. The ships are raised up and the bottle slightly magnifies it. The pinched sides give it a special frame and focus. Chemical bottles are special in their way too. They are rare, and the clean lines of the bottle set off the ship inside very nice-  ly. But, as you will see, even a gallon wine jug will command respect due the ability and artistic eye and hand of the builder. There are prune juice bottles, whiskey bottles, rum and vodka bottles, wine jugs, juice jugs and water jugs, chemical flasks and almost any clear glass container that will serve.

Off to the Grand Banks!

These Ship-in-a-Bottles *are bottles you do not have to uncork to enjoy the contents.* Set it on the mantle and stare at it for a moment. Feel the wind? Smell the sea? Look at that ship with bone in her teeth! Is it outward bound with trade goods for the east? Or is she coming home with a rich cargo of whale oil or spices and silks? Let your eyes feast, and your mind run free.

Enjoy this collection

Leo P. Convery

Real fine tarred marlin rope-work

The classic bottle is the Haig and Haig pinch bottle. This fine 3 masted full rigged ship is bound out for the Indies. Note the fine rope cap made of tarred marlin line, **#1**

The Haig and Haig pinch bottle is bent up on the bottom and displays the vessel high as if mounted on a cresting wave. This great 3 masted bark is under full sail. **#2**

Another 3 masted ship sails on the cresting sea. These bottles all measure about 8 inches long by 4.5 inches tall. This one has a particularly good cap made of leather molded onto the neck. **#3**

This fine example of a 3 masted ship under full sail has a light house introduced and a very nice red enamel cap on the bottle. Look at the size of the vessels and the small neck of the bottle **#4**

The simple square bottle makes a good presentation, as there is little distortion from the glass. This example is a simpler model of a 3 masted bark with reefed tops and the others furled. The cork is the original bottle cork. In the top rear is a small tag with "Sailor Flint 39" on it. Possibly the maker in 1939 **#5**

This is another Haig and Haig pinch bottle. It is a very simple but graceful full rigged ship under full sail. The cork is the original stopper for the whiskey bottle and it is sealed with green wax. The sea is a very deep green, almost like grass **#6**

These next two ship in a bottles are contemporary, made in 1985 by Leon Bistour of Robin Hoods Bay, North Yorkshire, England

He is a prolific modeler. Mr. Bistour made similar models for Pussars Rum company store in the Virgin Islands. Pussars would send him all the bottles he could use. They are excellent well executed ships. This one is an upright. Both are the same ship, The "Richard", a Brig that carried coal between York and the Thames. It was sunk off Robin Hoods Bay in 1786. **#7**

This is one of Mr. Leon Bistour's best. Very well executed. Note the small ketch in the neck, and the Turk's head rope work. There is a message about the ship and its history on the bottom, and it is labeled in the neck under the ketch, "Made especially for Leo P. Convery, 1985. It is in a House of Lords Whiskey bottle. **#8**

This one is one of my favorites and one of the smallest. It is about 6 inches long. A three masted ship is being eased into port by a steam tug, belching black smoke. The old chemical bottle is a bit fogged and quite thick, so it distorts one's view slightly. The smoke is some sort of black wool like material. **#9**

This is a detail of the above, still hard to see the full hull of the small tug. The bottle is unique and the scene in very original. This was found in a Newport RI antique shop in the 70's.

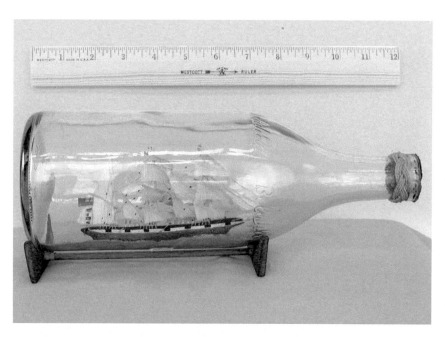

"Bobidilla y Cia" marks the bottom of this bottle and around the top. A very excellent model of a full rigged bark with all sails set. At 10.5 inches long it as one of the larger bottles. A Turk's head rope work decorates the bottle's neck. **#10**

This Schaeffer Bottle is a very unique. The back ground of 3 mountains, a small village, quay and rippled water. The ship is fairly simple but well made 3 masted bark with furled sails. The best part is the great tightly woven marlin rope-work cap. **#11**

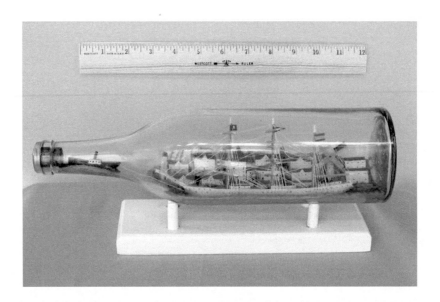

The red roofed village is very prominent. It has a lighthouse up near the neck and a windmill at the other end. The large white hulled ship is under tow by a small tug with a red stack. The tug sits high up in the neck of the bottle and a tow line drops down to the ship. **#12**

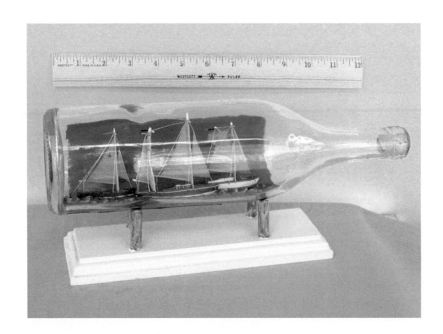

This is a much larger bottle. The models are marconi and gaff rigged. At the left end is a sloop, a ketch in the center and a gaff rig sloop to the right. An unusual setting. The back ground is painted blue, and the clay sea light green with white caps. Feel the wind! **#13**

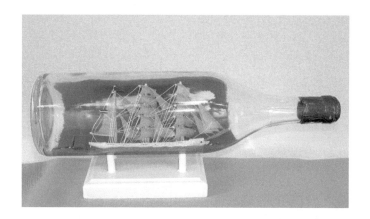 

This bottle is really great, the model is very nicely done and the whole is simple and understated. It is a very pleasing piece.

The backside of the bottle contains the original label. "Deutches Peppermint Liquor". The red seal seems to be original with the bottle. These bottles were carried around the world so it is hard to try to pin the origin country of the model to the bottle, **#14**

This old Prune juice bottle proves that any container will make a good receptacle for a ship model. The deep sea green is a bit hard to see through but I think this a very good piece. The model flies an American flag at the spanker gaff. **#15**

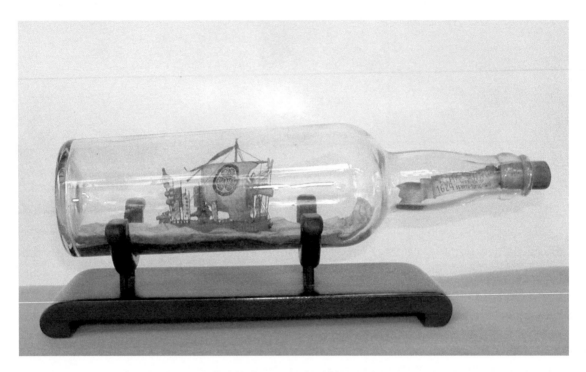

The "Atake-Maru" is one of the very best pieces. Very unusual and unique. It is a Japanese war ship with full ceremonial flags and shields. The sea is made with rice paper that has been treated with varnish or shellac to give it body and stability. The stand is very attractive and simple. A banner curls from the neck and states "Atake-Maru, war-ship 1624, Iemitu-Tokugawa" **#16**

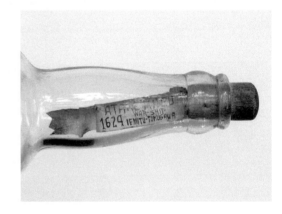

The Tokugawa Family Crest is prominent on the sail.

This is a large and most unusual bottle. The ship is magnificent. There is a volcano and a lighthouse that light up inside the bottle. The back of the bottle shows the wires, the battery case, the switch, and the erupting volcano. The bottle measures 14 in. long by 4 ½ in. wide. **#17**

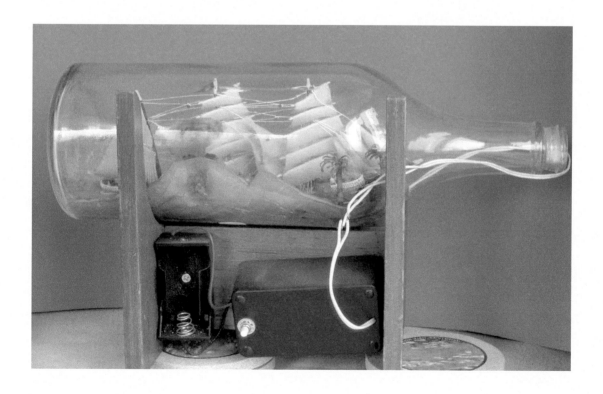

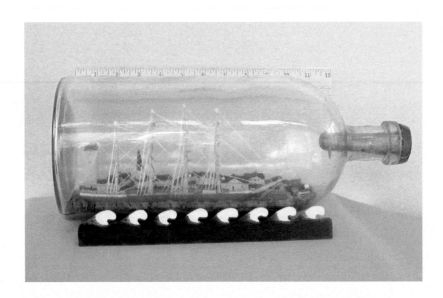

This is a large water jug or chemical bottle. It measures 14 inches long by 5 ½ in. wide. The four mast-ed ship is tied up to a quay in a small village with a church and light house. The stopper is loose but has a stake through it so the stopper cannot be withdrawn. **#18**

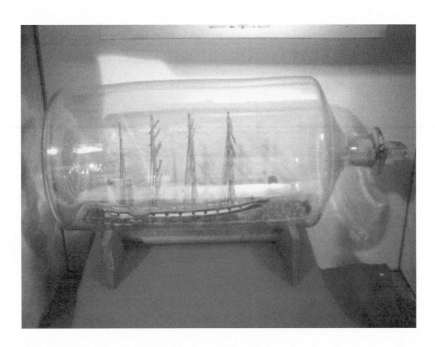

Another large, 13in. long by 5.25in. wide, chemical bottle. This is about the third bottle that I acquired in the early 60's. The bottle is stopped by the original glass stopper. It is a great piece, very simply exe-cuted and has good detail. An unusual Bottle and ship. **#19**

This is an extremely large jug, measuring 16 in. long by 7 in. wide. It is a contemporary model. The bottom of the bottle is inscribed " Emma C. Berry" " launched Noank , Conn. 1866" length 45' 9"-beam 14' 8" draft 5'3" status Mystic Seaport exhibit, scale 10=1in. finished Dec. 1981, 8 of 8 Gilbert J. Charbonnau **#20**

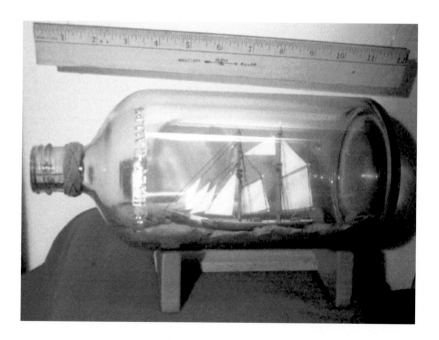

A smaller 10 in. Long by 4 ½ wide water jug. The jug has one half gallon on the shoulder. The vessel is a schooner with typical rig for fishing off the Grand Banks. She is passing a light house. The bottom is inscribed "J. H. Manley, 1991" Note the Turks head around the neck. **#21**

This great gallon jug must have been full of "grappa". Two full rigged ships beat to the harbor entrance, headed out to sea. The small white houses must have been along the Italian coast. Note the twin light towers on the jetties and the trees in the back. A very unusual piece. **#22**

This is an unusual 6 sided bottle. The heavy glass and the angle of the sides joining make it difficult to photo the very nice 3 masted ship and detailed village. The original cork is the stopper. **#23**

 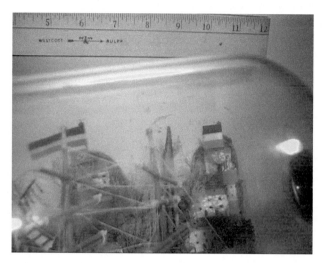

This great little bottle was found on Nantucket during the summer of 2000. it is very unusual because of the flags and banners. I believe it must have been built in the 1920's or early 30's. It is very well executed and very busy little village. There is a windmill and a slim lighthouse, and little red roofed village homes scattered about. The flags are German and the detail shows small red flags with swastika's. The trees are bits of brown tops of grass and are shedding some what. The bottle's neck is painted with gold and a cork stops the neck. **#24**

This is another very special model. The bottle is a Teachers scotch bottle. The ship is 4 masted and with full sails. The bottle's neck has a Turk's head of cotton line. **#25**

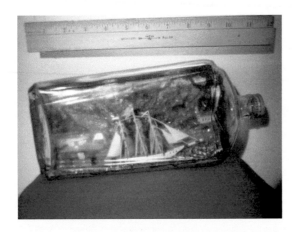 

The two ships in bottles above were found at different times in England.

They are both in very similar Consolidated Distilleries bottles. Both are detailed with intricate backgrounds. The one on the left is a northern scene, the right has palm trees and lush greenery like a tropical island. Note the very small bottleneck openings. It took a great deal of work to build and finish these very elaborate ship-in-a-bottles. **#26   #27**

Another well made model in an oval bottle. The ship and village are very well done. The ship is up against the quay and the small village homes are prominent. The end of the bottle is capped with a very well done rope work of tarred marlin. The oval shape of the bottle makes the interior display easier to see. **#28**

This little ship in the bottle lamp was given to me at about the age of 5. It has been with me ever since. This small lamp stands about 14 inches tall. It has soft pleats around the glass bottom. I think it was made on Martha's Vineyard in the early 30's. by an old man called Capt. Ivory. He lived in a cat boat up on dry land and built ship in bottles to sell. **#29**

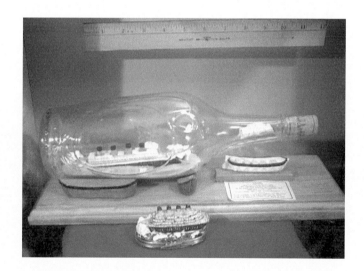

TheTitanic on her way to the bottom! After a visit to the Savannah Marine Museum, where I saw a ship in a bottle of the Titanic., I built one. An iceberg sits up in the neck. A lifeboat under it. Lifeboat hulls support the bottle. A small 3 inch Limoges box of the titanic sits out in front. **#30**

A Johnnie Walker Scotch bottle is home to this four stack cruise ship. The ship is passing headland with a light house on the side of it. The bottle is glued to its stand. **#31**

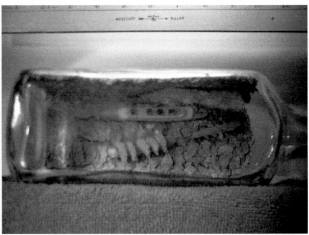

This is an unusual bottle. The scenery is clay laid up on the side and bottom, with a small island represented in the front corner. Most of the ships could have easily passed through the neck of the bottle. It is the variety and number and detail that make it interesting. There is a sizeable cruise ship, a 5 masted square rigger with full sail, a five masted lumber schooner, a 3 masted schooner, One, with two masts and a small sloop. These can be seen from the top down view of the lower photo. The bottle is square with no markings. **#32**

Air Attack! Is the title of this bottle, a British destroyer steams out in a sea of cotton. Orange cotton simulates smoke streaming from her stacks and powder burst from her guns. This is so over done as to be amusing if not ugly. It is also the only cheater I have seen. The bottom quarter of the bottle has been cut off, and the plaster straps around the bottle conceal it. There is a light under it too. **#33**

Not all things in bottles are ships, as this British spitfire proves. In a pint size Haig and Haig Scotch bottle. This is most likely the air cover for the destroyer above. **#34**

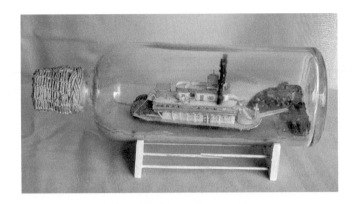

This very unique bottle with a Mississippi paddle wheel driven river boat was found in England. Note the intricate rope work on the bottle neck. The detail shows the deck support and the paddle wheel. The model seems to be built out of wood and paper. It is just very unusual to see this type of vessel in a bottle. **#35**

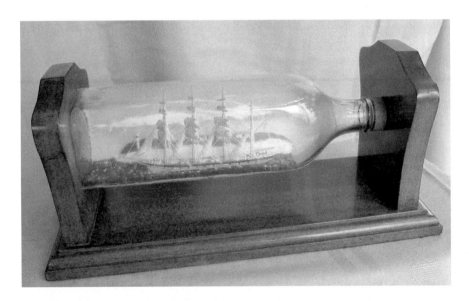

Here is a very fine 4 masted bark is in an unusual wood holder. The base of what might be a Johnnie Walker Scotch bottle has been carved into the wood upright. The model faces to the rear of the bottle. Most US builders put the ship in Stern first, so the bow is facing the neck. **#36**

This bottle illustrates the detail of why the Haig and Haig pinch bottle is a classic for showing off a model. The ship is a simple model but the rope work cap makes it very special. **#37**

The very intricate rope work is made from tarred marlin. which was made from jute. This is a very lost art today. How did they get the weaving tight as it shrunk around the narrower neck? It is almost crochet work

The Ships in each Bottle are very unique and take a great deal of time to execute. After all the effort that goes into the inside of a bottle, I am always amazed to find the really good rope work on the neck or some other really unique decoration to set the bottle model off. Here are a few of the best.

This cap is on bottle number 11. It is very heavily tarred marlin, very tight and has a unique stand up pattern..

This cap adorns bottle number 28. It is similar in material as number 12, but the weave is tight, and the tar heavy. Excellent rope work

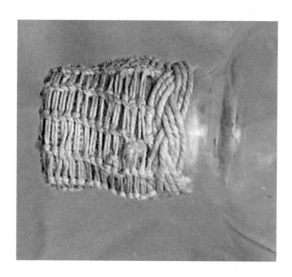

This is from the Paddle wheeled River boat bottle, number 35. The rope appears to be cotton twine and is good work, but I think a bit less skilled than the other two.

The dark red cap is a very different approach to capping the neck of a bottle.

It appears to be a piece of leather that has been shrunk onto and over the cap. The deep red color is very attractive. This is on Bottle number 3

This knot, on the neck of number 10, is more typical of the newer built models. The Turks head is not an easy knot to master but compared to the above intricate marlin work, it is an easier execution and adds a nice nautical finish.

The Turk's head knot surrounds the neck and overlaps the cork stopper, another interesting way to finish off the bottle. The ship is excellent work, the knot loses in comparison to the others above. But it is a nice finish to bottle no. 1

"The Cover Bottle"

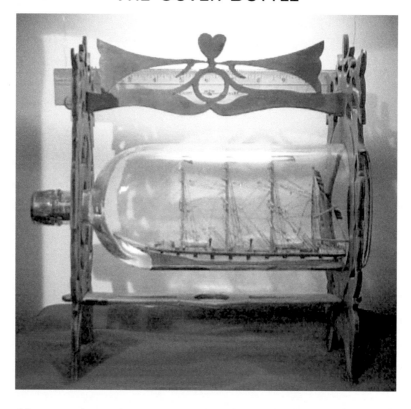

This bottle was found in an antique shop near Exeter, Devon, England.

The piece is outstanding from any standpoint. The bottle shape, the four masted ship and the scroll stand all meld to make this piece pleasing to any beholder. The stand is 1/8 inch plywood which has been stained and fits by interlocking pieces that are pegged to hold it together. **#39**

THE SHIP-IN-A-BOTTLE

Identification of the basic sail configurations of sailing vessels

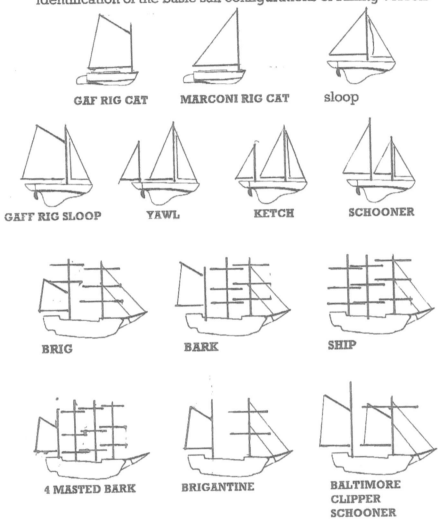

These are the basic sailing vessel rigs. In the 1800's there were innumerable variations depending on the hull, the purpose of the vessel, speed or cargo capacity, or war, and even the individual master of the ship. Sail plans on the great India trading ships and clipper ships were more complicated and numerous. Sails were added to the tops of the masts, end of the booms and anywhere canvas could be stretched between all of the spars. Today most sailing vessels use the fore and aft sail configuration as they help in beating to wind ward, something the old square riggers were not noted for doing well. The great clipper ships still hold some of the fastest world sailing speed records today.

.

Sources of Interest , modelers, web sites, books.

How To Books

SHIPS-IN-BOTTLES- A step by step guide to a venerable nautical craft by Commander Donald Hubard, USN (Ret.)

Ships in Bottles by guy DeMarco Shiffer Publishing Atglen, PA

Associations

Don Hubbard, Pres.

Ship-In-Bottles Association of America

      P.O. Box 180550

      Coranado, CA 92178

Dutch Assoc. of Ship in Bottles   **http://home.uwnet.nl~hongste/sibnl.htm**

Modelers- email, web sites

David Smith   **dsresrch@fundy.net**   Also links to other sites

Ichimura Shinzo   **http://www3.justnet.ne.jp/~itisin**

Eduardo Raffalli   **www.7.50megs.com/eddys.html**

Gilbert Charboneau- custom modeler

      http://lincoln.midcoast.com/~gilships/commissioning.html

Artem Popov, Moscow   **www.shipinbottle.ru/artempopov**

Joe Register- W. VA   **http://pages.prodigy.net/markand** ***

Ralph Preston   **http://natosongs.com/hit-the-bottle.html/Ralph_preston**

Bill Lucas   how to book   **www.lucasshipinbottles.com/**

Web sites with good links to other modelers

http://lincoln.midcoast.com/~gilships/favoritelinks.html

http://user.fundy.net/fpweb/2-hist.html

http://sailing.aout.com/recreation/sailing/cs/shipsinbottles/index_2htm

MUSEUMS AROUND THE WORLD

U.S.

New Bedford Whaling Museum- new Bedford MA

Peabody- Essex Museum, Salem Mass

Mystic Seaport, Mystic Conn.

Mariners Museum- Norfolk VA

Whaling Museum, Cold Springs Harbor, New York.

OTHER-

Musees de St. Malo, St. Malo, France.

Smithsonian   Washington, D. C.

Struer Museum, Sondergrade 23, Struer, Denmark

Flaskeskibsmuseet, Smedegade 22, Aeroskobing, Denmark

Marstal Sofartsmuseum, Prinsgade 2-4, Marstal, Denmark

Osaka Bottleship Mini Museum. Kaiyukan Entrance Bldg. 10 kaigandori1-Chome, Minatao-ku, Osaka, Japan

Yokohama Maritime Museum 1-1, Minato-Mirai 2-chome,nishi-ku, Yokohama, Japan.

Glasgow Art Gallery and Museum, Glasgow, Scotland

The National Maritime Museum, Greenwich, England.

Museo Maritimo, Barcelona, Spain

Nationsl Scheepvaartmuseum, Antwerp, Belgium

OTHER THINGS ARE PUT INTO BOTTLES TOO

These are called Whimseys or whimsical things in a bottle. So it was not just the boat lovers and seaman that practiced the craft. The varieties of these too, are infinite.

Printed in the United States
by Baker & Taylor Publisher Services